DATE DUE

GAYLORD			PRINTED IN U.S.A

EVENING TRAIN

Books by Denise Levertov

Poetry

The Double Image
Here and Now
Overland to the Islands
With Eyes at the Back of Our Heads
The Jacob's Ladder
O Taste and See
The Sorrow Dance
Relearning the Alphabet
To Stay Alive
Footprints
The Freeing of the Dust
Life in the Forest
Collected Earlier Poems 1940–1960
Candles in Babylon
Poems 1960–1967
Oblique Prayers
Poems 1968–1972
Breathing the Water
A Door in the Hive
Evening Train

Prose

New & Selected Essays

Translations

Guillevic/Selected Poems
Joubert/Black Iris (Copper Canyon Press)

EVENING
TRAIN

DENISE
LEVERTOV

A NEW DIRECTIONS BOOK

Grateful acknowledgment is made to the editors and publishers of magazines in which some of the poems in this collection first appeared: *American Poetry Review, Am Here Forum, Amicus Journal, Aril/Cross Currents, Cafe Review, Cantielevers, The Catholic Worker, Common Knowledge, In Context, Mississippi Valley Review, New American Writing, Northlight* (England), *Private, Range, Seneca Quarterly, Sojourner, Storm Warning, Verve, Zyzzyva.* Some poems also appeared in the anthologies *After the Storm* and *The WPFW Poetry Anthology.* The poems in Section I, Lake Mountain Moon, were published in a limited edition by Tangram Press, which also, separately, published as a limited edition chapbook the suite of poems 'Embracing the Multipede.'

Author's Note: A number of these poems were written at the Rockefeller Foundation's Villa Serbelloni, at Bellagio, Lake Como. I shall always recall my five weeks there with joy and gratitude. The 'Two Magnets' section of this book is dedicated to the memory of Roberto Celli the then director, and to Gianna Celli.

Manufactured in the United States of America
New Directions Books are printed on acid-free paper
First published clothbound in 1992
Published simultaneously in Canada by Penguin Books Canada Limited

Library of Congress Cataloging-in-Publication Data
Levertov, Denise, 1923–
      Evening train / Denise Levertov.
         p.   cm.
      Includes index.
      ISBN 0–8112–1219–X (alk. paper)
      I. Title.
PS3562.E88E94 1992
811'.54—dc20   92–20385
                                                                        CIP

New Directions Books are published for James Laughlin
by New Directions Publishing Corporation,
80 Eighth Avenue, New York 10011

Contents

I

Lake Mountain Moon

I was welcomed here—clear gold
of late summer, of opening autumn,
the dawn eagle sunning himself on the highest tree,
the mountain revealing herself unclouded, her snow
tinted apricot as she looked west,
tolerant, in her steadfastness, of the restless sun
forever rising and setting.
                    Now I am given
a taste of the grey foretold by all and sundry,
a grey both heavy and chill. I've boasted I would not care,
I'm London-born. And I won't. I'll dig in,
into my days, having come here to live, not to visit.
Grey is the price
of neighboring with eagles, of knowing
a mountain's vast presence, seen or unseen.

The mountain comes and goes
on the horizon,

a rhythm elusive as that of a sea-wave
higher than all the rest, riding to shore
flying its silver banners—

you count to seven, but no,
its measure
slips by you with each recurrence.

The mountain absent,
a remote folk-memory.

The peninsula
vanished, hill, trees—
gone, shoreline
a rumour.

And we equate
God with these absences—
Deus absconditus.
But God

is imaged
as well or better
in the white stillness

resting everywhere,

giving to all things
an hour of Sabbath,

no leaf stirring,
the hidden places

tranquil in solitude.

Though the mountain's the same warm-tinted ivory
as the clouds (as if a red ground had been laid beneath
not quite translucent white) and though the clouds
disguise its shoulders, and rise tall to left and right,
and soften the pale summit with mist,

                                   yet one perceives
the massive presence, obdurate, unconcerned
among those filmy guardians.

Today the mountain
is cloud,
pale cone of shadow
veiled by a paler scrim—

majestic presence become
one cloud among others,
humble vapor,
barely discernible,

like the archangel walking
with Tobias on dusty roads.

St. Simon Heron,
standing, standing, standing
upon his offshore pillar,

suddenly, subtly
dips his head to drink,
Three, then a fourth,
and more times, that legato
arabesque of the neck,
the small head almost a serpent's,
smoothly one with its flexible stem.
Body and tall legs
move not an inch.
      Hunger,
thirst, fulfillment
are ripples that lap his surface;
his patience absorbs them.
Time does not pass, for him;
it is the lake, and full, and still,
and he has all of it, and wades to strike
when he will upon his fish.

Elegantly gray, the blue heron
rises from perfect stillness on wide wings,
   flies a few beats
 sideways,
    trails his feet in the lake,
 and rises again to circle
from marker to marker (the posts
that show where the bottom shelves downward)
choosing:
and lands on the floating dock where the gulls cluster—

a tall prince come down from the castle to walk,
proud and awkward, in the market square,
while squat villagers
break off their deals
and look askance.

Here comes the moon,
bright rim
slicing importantly
through windrows of
grey thistledown cloud just losing
their sundown flush.

The last warm day, I caught,
almost unnoticing,
      that high shrilling like thin
wires of spun silver, glint
of wheeling flight—some small tribe
leaving.
               That night
the moon was full; by morning
autumn had come.

1

Moon, wisp of opal fire, then slowly
revealed as orb arising,
still half-hidden; the dark
bulk of the wooded ridge defined
by serrations of pine and fir against
this glow
        that begins to change
from lambent red to a golden
pervasive mist of light as the whole
fullness of moon
floats clear of the hill.

2

Risen, the gold moon
will shrink and blanch
but for now, still
low in the sky,

her pallor is veiled
as if by a net of
gilded gossamer

and the path she has laid down
over the ripples of
dark lake water

is gold unalloyed.

A gull far-off
rises and falls, arc of a breath,
two sparrows pause on the telephone wire,
chirp a brief interchange, fly back to the ground,
the bus picks up one passenger and zooms on up the hill,
across the water the four poplars
conceal their tremor, feet together, arms pressed to their sides,
behind them the banked conifers dark and steep;
my peartree drops a brown pear from its inaccessible height
into the bramble and ivy tangle, grey sky
whitens a little, now one can see vague forms of cloud
pencilled lightly across it.
This is the day that the Lord hath made,
let us rejoice and be glad in it.

Perhaps one day I shall let myself
approach the mountain—
hear the streams which must flow down it,
lie in a flowering meadow, even
touch my hand to the snow.
Perhaps not. I have no longing to do so.
I have visited other mountain heights.
This one is not, I think, to be known
by close scrutiny, by touch of foot or hand
or entire outstretched body; not by any
familiarity of behavior, any acquaintance
with its geology or the scarring roads
humans have carved in its flanks.
This mountain's power
lies in the open secret of its remote
apparition, silvery low-relief
coming and going moonlike at the horizon,
always loftier, lonelier, than I ever remember.

II

The Two Magnets

The Two Magnets

Where broken gods, faded saints, (powerful in antique presence
as old dancers with straight backs, loftily confident,
or old men in threadbare wellcut coats) preside casually
over the venerable conversations of cypress and olive,
there intrudes, like a child interrupting, tugging at my mind,
incongruous, persistent,
the image of young salmon in round ponds at the hatchery
across an ocean and a continent, circling
with muscular swiftness—tints of green, pink, blue,
glowing mysteriously through slate gray, under trees
unknown here, whose names I forget because
they were unknown to me too when I was young.

And there on the western edge of America—home to me now,
and calling me with this image of something I love,
yet still unknown—I dream of cathedrals,
of the worn stone of human centuries.
Guarded by lions with blunted muzzles
or griffins verdant with moss, gateposts open in me
to effaced avenues.
Part of me lives under nettle-grown foundations.
Part of me wanders west and west, and has reached
the edge of the mist where salmon wait the day
when something shall lift them and give them to deeper waters.

Tattooed in black and gold, lichened nymphs,
sentinels faithful to their garden wall,
face the impertinent back of a new villa,
their view of the lake usurped.

Stele

(I-II c. B.C.)

They part at the edge of substance.
Henceforth, he will be shadow
in a land of shadow.
And she—she too will be going
slowly down a road of cloud,
weightless, untouched, untouching.
This is the last crossroad.
Her right hand and his left
are clasped, but already,
muffled in his acceptance of fate,
his attention recedes from her.
Her left hand rises, fingertips trace
the curve of his warm face
as it cools and fades.
He has looked down his road,
he is ready to go, not willingly
yet without useless resistance.
She too accepts the truth, there is no way back,
but she has not looked, yet, at the path
accorded to her. She has not given herself,
not yet, to her shadowhood.

Play with a few decades, shift them:
try to imagine Ruskin in the New World,
walking with John Muir in the wilderness.

He, whose enraptured first sight of the Alps
transformed him, that meek Protestant Sunday
when he and Mama and Papa and dull cousin Mary
were patiently waiting the secular week's beginning
before attempting the sights,
                          but all unawares
came face to face
with the sublime—unmistakeably not clouds,
surpassing all that engravings had promised,
floating west of Schaffhausen, sharp, *tinged with rose—*
far into blue—suddenly—beyond!

—changed him from docile prig (poor child: he was 14 and knew
so much and so little) to a man of passion,
whatever his failings.

Imagine him in Yosemite. Would loyalties already divided
—Rock Simple or Rock Wrought,
strata of mountains, strata of human craft,
tools of Geology or tools of Art—have split him?
Would wilderness, legends unknown, or if known offering
no toe-hold for his mind's expectant footing,
have swept him wholly into its torrents of non-human grandeur?

Or wouldn't Art have pulled him back in the end
to layered history felt in the bones,
(even Geology a fraction of that insistence, loved
for its poetry of form, color, textures,
not as a scientist loves it)?
Back to where human hands created

rich tessellations or the *shadowy Rialto*
threw its colossal curve slowly
forth . . . that strange curve, so delicate,
so adamantine, strong as a mountain cavern,
graceful as a bow just bent—?

Back to where Nature—even the Alps, still so remote,
unsung through so many centuries—

lay in the net or nest of perception,
seen then re-seen, recognized, wrought in myth.

A Little Visit to Doves and Chickens

For Page Smith

Demure and peaceful, quiet above
the crooning chickens (who peck and strut,
equally peaceful in winter sun, a level below them,
as if on the ground-floor of a two-storey house),
the doves
are softly pale: gray warmed by brown;
and each one wears a collar, narrow and black
as the velvet ribbon girls and dowagers
used to clasp at the throat with a diamond.
Unlike their cousins the city pigeons,
they don't seem obsessed by sex or food,
don't chase one another in circles,
don't keep talking. They are as calm
in motion as in repose.
                              The chickens meanwhile
remind me of wealthy peasants
in an ancient culture—their rustic finery, gold,
scarlet, opulent umber, brighter and just as beautiful
as the doves' patrician sobriety, and their manners
good but less formal. Their comforts
are earned by their labors. One wonders
if from the doves also their keeper extracts a tithe,
or retains them merely to be
their dreamy selves.

No, there's no moral nor irony
lurking among these words, no message—
unless the sense
                    that it's pleasant to visit a while
                    a modest, indeed a minute, poultry yard
                    where such content may be witnessed
                    and even a pair of guineafowl don't seem nervous

is itself a message simply because
it's wistful, the leisure of mind
to lean on the fence and simply look, and not feel
the need to press for a subtext, being so rare.

The Composition

(*Woman at the Harpsichord,*
Emmanuel de Witte, 1617–1692
Musée des Beaux Arts, Montreal)

For Jean Joubert
and for Howard Fussiner

Two rooms away, seen through the open door,
the servant-maid raises her head to listen,
times the strokes of her broom to the music's crisp
golden wavelets. Autumn sun
and shadows well-defined overlay the floortiles,
antiphonal transverse strips over squares
of white and black. Filtered through little panes
in long and lofty windows, the light
hints at green in its morning pallor. But red,
red is the lord of color here: the draperies,
bedside carpet, ceiling-beams, elaborate
hanging lamp, a chair, all these and more
are a glowing Indian red; and red above all,
with its canopy, valance, ample curtains,
the big four-poster. Up and dressed, the young wife,
(white cap and dimly auburn skirts, red jacket
basqued with ermine-tips) is playing
the harpsichord, beginning the day with delight,
while snug, still, in the bed's half-dark reclines
the young husband, leaning his head on one hand,
intently, blissfully, watching and listening.
A human scene: apex of civilized joy, attained
in Holland, the autumn of 1660, never surpassed, probably
never to be matched.
                    But if
the same scene had been painted differently—
not only with other colors but from another
distance, perspectives differently disposed, more curves,
less play of severe rectangles if it had been

24

a composition that lacked this austere
counterpoint of forms which evoke,
in brave resplendent red, the very
twang and trill and wiry
ground bass of the notes ringing forth
under her fingers—if it had been
reduced to anecdote—we'd never have known
that once, in eternity,
this peaceful joy had blessed an autumnal morning.

III

Ancient Airs

A face ages quicker than a mind.

And thighs, arms, breasts,
take on an air of indifference.
Heart's desire has wearied them, they chose to forget
whatever they once promised.

But mind and heart continue
their eager conversation,
they argue, they share epiphanies,
sometimes all night they raise
antiphonal laments.

Face and body have betrayed them,

they are alone together,
unsure how to proceed.

1 Mysterious Movement

Though no wind is blowing, the lake,
        as if to reënact the remote day
        when, as a journeying river, it first flowed
        into the long hollow of its bed
        and met the embracing shores
        and could go no further,
is pressing strongly, darkly,
southward in fading light, this waning hour
near the close of the year—

although it can go no further.

2 Midwinter

A sky stained
even at midmorning
with the water and blood of daybreak . . .

And the mountain,
strangely approachable
this winter day,
has moved forward into the middle distance,
humbly letting valleys and dark
seams of rock be perceived,
like a woman not trying to hide
her loss of youth from the light.
Her snows are gray.

30

Ancient Airs and Dances

I

I knew too well
what had befallen me
when, one night, I put my lips to his wineglass
after he left—an impulse I thought was locked away with a smile
into memory's museum.

When he took me to visit friends and the sea, he lay
asleep in the next room's dark where the fire
rustled all night; and I, from a warm bed, sleepless,
watched through the open door
that glowing hearth, and heard,
drumming the roof, the rain's
insistent heartbeat.

Greyhaired, I have not grown wiser,
unless to perceive absurdity
is wisdom. A powerless wisdom.

II

Shameless heart! Did you not vow to learn
            stillness from the heron,
            quiet from the mists of fall,
            and from the mountain—what was it?
            Pride? Remoteness?
You have forgotten already!
And now you clamor again
like an obstinate child demanding attention,
interrupting study and contemplation.
You try my patience. Bound as we are
together for life, must you now,
so late in the day, go bounding sideways,
trying to drag me with you?

Reinforced though it was
with stoic strapping,
my heart was breaking again. Damn!
Just when I had so much to do,
a list as long as your arm.
The world news slithered
toward the probable worst
of a lifetime's bad news,
and as for me (as if in that shadow it mattered—
but it did) in two day's time
I'd be saying goodbye to someone I thought of
'day and night,' as I'd not been planning to think
of anyone ever again.

I'd believed it would hold, yes,
I'd considered my serviceable heart
long-since well-mended,
and equal to what demands
might still confront it.
And hadn't I written, still longer ago,
that these metaphorical hearts, although
they 'break for nothing,' do so
in surface fissures only, a web
of hairline fractures, the way
old pieplates do, rimmed with a blue design
as if someone had pressed them all round
with tines of a fork well-dipped in indigo?
All true enough, but surely by now
mine, though made like such plates
for use, not show, must need
those clamps of metal with which
cracked vessels of finer porcelain are held.
For the moment I'd have to make do
with tape and crossed fingers.

32

Away from home,
the reality of home
evades me. Chairs,
sofa, table, a cup—
I can enumerate objects
one by one, but they're inventory,
not Gestalt. This house
I've stayed in often before,
the open suitcase,
my friends who live here,
that's what's real.
And that face
so vivid to me these past three months
evades me too: the shape
of his head, or
color of his eyes appear
at moments, but I can't
assemble feature with feature.
I seem to have landed
upon this *now*
as if on a mid-ocean island,
past and future two continents, both
lost in immense distance,
the mist and seasons
of months at sea—the voyage
from yesterday to today.

IV

Flowers of Sophia

Peak upon peak, brown, dustily gold, crowded,
sharp juttings, razorbacks, angular undulations,
so many we seem not to move above them, confusion
of multitudinous upthrust forms, pushing
against one another, surging.
                              Valley forests
look from the air like dark green water,
but if there are lakes
they are hidden. A dry country
unless when the snows melt.

But at last
when a true lake shows itself
it is blue, blue, blue,
a cupful of sky.

Tiepolo clouds—
tinge of beige in diaphanous shadow
over cornfields and western bluffs
where no one has seen
how they hang also above
ascensions, veils,
ecstatic saints and the heads
of cherubim . . .

Bloodred, viridian, poison aqua:
round mineral pools or pits in the Nullarbor.
My photo, taken through scratched glass from the air,
was to have been a gift for an artist son,
but came out blurred and pale
and was never given.
                    Years later,
flying above a different desert,
I see with mind's eye the painting I imagined
he might have made from the pattern's
aboriginal mystery.

Sky-wave breaks
in surf, and leaves
the lace of it to border
an obscure, etherial,
sinuous coastline—

phosphorescent for that lingering
instant which is to us
time immemorial.

In this dark I rest,
unready for the light which dawns
day after day,
eager to be shared.
Black silk, shelter me.
I need
more of the night before I open
eyes and heart
to illumination. I must still
grow in the dark like a root
not ready, not ready at all.

Night's broken wing
and its wide untorn one
hobble across the paling sky
dropping black feathers down on black trees.
Day is still forming itself.
This is the gap,
the time between the sagacious, taciturn wolf
and the plain dog who will yap into place
when dawn has flared and faded.

On the Eve

For Melanie

The moon was white
in the stillness. Daylight
changed without moving,
a hint of sundown
stained the sky. We walked
the short grass,
the dry ground of the hill,
beholding
the tinted west. We talked
of change in our lives. The moon
tuned its whiteness a tone higher.

Dreaming the sea that
                    lies beyond me
I have enough depth
                    to know I am shallow.

I have my pools, my bowls
                    of rock I flow
into and fill, but I must
                    brim my own banks, persist,
vanish at last in greater flood
                        yet still within it
follow my task,
            dreaming towards
the calling sea.

Brother Ivy

Between road and sidewalk, the broadleafed ivy,
unloved, dusty, littered, sanctuary of rats,
gets on with its life. New leaves shine gaily
among dogged older ones
that have lost their polish.
It does not require appreciation. The foliage
conceals a brown tangle of stems
thick as a mangrove swamp; the roots
are spread tenaciously. Unwatered
throughout the long droughts, it simply
grips the dry ground by the scruff of the neck.

I am not its steward.
If we are siblings, and I
my brother's keeper therefore,
the relation is reciprocal. The ivy
meets its obligation by pure
undoubtable being.

The neighbor's Black Labrador, his owners
out at work, unconscious anyone
is watching him, rises again and again
on hind legs to bend with his paws
the figtree's curving branches
and reach the sweet figs with his black lips.

The polar she-bear, dirty ivory
against the blue-white steep
slope of ice
rolls and slides like a cub,
happy to stretch cramped limbs after four
months in the stuffy den;
but quickly lopes
upward with toed-in undulant grace
back to the bleating summons
of three new bears, their first time out,
hind feet still in the tunnel,
black astonished eyes regarding
their mother at play, black noses
twitching, smelling
strange wonders of air and light.

Flax, chicory, scabious—
flowers with ugly names,
they grow in waste ground, sidewalk edges,
fumes, grime, trash.
Each kind has a delicate form, distinctive;
it would be pleasant to draw them.
All are a dreamy blue,
a gentle mysterious blue,
wise beyond comprehension.

V

Evening Train

Over gin and tonic (an unusual treat) the ancient poet
haltingly—not because mind and memory
   falter, but because language, now,
   weary from so many years
   of intense partnership,
   comes stiffly to her summons,
   with unsure footing—
recounts, for the first time in my hearing, each step
of that graceful sarabande, her husband's
last days, last minutes, fifteen years ago.

She files her belongings freestyle, jumbled
in plastic bags—poems, old letters, ribbons,
old socks, an empty pictureframe;
but keeps her fifty years of marriage wrapped, flawless,
in something we sense and almost see
diaphanous as those saris one can pass through a wedding ring.

He saw the dark as a ragged garment
spread out to air.
Through its rents and moth-holes
the silver light came pouring.

As if we were sitting as we have done so often,
over a cup of tea, and I knew how
to read the leaves, let me look closely into
this card you have sent, this image you say
holds for you something you feel is yourself.
A woman sits outdoors by a white-cloth'd table
(blue in shadow); but it's not a café;
there are columns, masonry, perhaps a ruin behind her,
and also a stretch of open lawn or pasture,
and trees beyond. She has opened—a parasol?
or an umbrella? There's enough light to suggest
a parasol, but the coat she wears
is not for summer: passionate red is muted
almost to russet, and high collar, sleeves
that narrow from elbow to wrist, imply weight,
warm cloth. Yet the silken shelter's pale cerulean,
shot with gold, seems too light for rain.
Perhaps it is rainbow weather, flying showers
on a gleaming day in spring.
Not a young girl any more, this woman's
fresh color and shining hair are not yet
beginning to fade; but in her eyes one sees
knowledge, though in their clear, steady,
almost challenging gaze there's a certain innocence;
and her lips are firmly closed. Bareheaded,
(despite her coat) she is quietly seated,
not poised to leave; one arm rests on the chair's
green embracing arm.   Most notable in this portrait:
her solitude. She may or may not be waiting for someone;
whether or not, she looks out from the picture-plane
not at the painter but straight through time
at me looking back at her. She's not sad,
not angry, not joyful: but open, open
to what shall befall.

53

                    The image is only
a detail, fragment of a larger whole.
The context might change my reading. Companions
perhaps are nearby, unseen by us; perhaps she too
doesn't see them. The place she is in
might be defined if one saw the rest of the painting.
One might deduce from it why she is there,
where she will go. But the more I look, the more
I perceive what her eyes express: it's courage.
That's what told me this woman is innocent but not ignorant.
Courage knows the price of living. Courage itself
is a form of innocence, of trust or faith.
Your sense of being portrayed no doubt refers
to less than this; to her solitude, it may be.
It's against the rules to tell your own fortune,
and I, after all, am able only to descry
the images in the leaves, not to construe their meaning.
Some day one of us may discover the painting's whereabouts,
see the whole of it. Then we'll divine
what fortune her gaze betokens.

Becca. Each washday,
steamy scullery, yellow soap-smell, whites
boiled in the copper. Becca brandishing
a stick, huge spoon to stir the bubbling
soup of linens.
A child had best keep out of the way.
And skreak of the mangle turning
hurt to hear.
Outdoors, though,
clotheslines made streets across the lawn,
walled with sheets, a billowing village.
Becca, bandy-legged, sturdy
under the weight, brought forth
the round wicker basket,
stretched wet
huge arms to the line to peg,
with gypsy pegs that stuffed
her apron pockets, more and more
clean clothes, mangle-wrung,
and the washday wind
slapped them, slapped
me as I dodged from door to invisible door, Becca
shouting, but not at me,
she was deaf I think, I think we never
exchanged a word, she just
appeared and then it was washday, but not
after I was six, perhaps five, perhaps four, yes,
early—for me she existed
at our washtub only, and in our garden,
with no in-between, no home, no story,
toothlessly smiling (not at me).
Lodged in my head
forever, primordial. Becca.
Known. Unknown.

You danced ahead of me, I took
none of those last steps with you
when your *enchainement* led you
uphill to the hospital and a death sentence
or before that when language
twirled round and tripped your voice.
Dancers must learn to walk
slowly across a stage, unfaltering;
we practiced that, long ago.
You faltered, but only in the wings,
that week when *timor mortis*
lunged at you. And you shook off
that devouring terror, held up
your head, straightened
your back, and moved in grace
(they tell me—I was not at your side
but far away,
intent on a different music)
into the light of that last stage,
a hospice garden, where you could say,
breathing the ripened fragrance of August mornings,
'yes, and evenings too are beautiful.'

Half memory of what my mother
at over ninety could still see
clear in mind's eye, transferring,
like earrings or brooches,
her lapidary trove
into my vision; half imprint
of that charcoal-burner with his boy,
gazing at thickets towering up
around the sleeping palace
in my childhood treasure of treasures,
Dulac's Perrault,
                    I carry
into this alien epoch, year by year,
the presence of that venerable great-
or great-great uncle to whom,
precociously observant five-year-old,
she was taken one summer day
and told to remember always
that *he* could remember Waterloo,
when he was a drummer-boy, a lad
of twelve perhaps, and how Napoleon—
Boney, the bogeyman disobedient children
were threatened with—rode off on his mountainous
black horse.

The ancient's dark nets were spread
before his cottage; drowsing waves
lapped the Welsh strand and his beached coracle,
reflections wavering on the brilliant whitewash.
White hair grew to his shoulders, kneebritches left
his brown legs bare, his feet were bare.
Indoors, the earth floor, hard as flagstones,
had for ornament patterns he drew
with the staining juice of a certain plant.

        I perceive, seeing him there,
his life, glimpsed that day and held
in the amber pendant I inherit, belongs
to any of several centuries, though now
it has no place except in me, as if memory travelled
fingertip to outstretched fingertip
across the longest lives, an electric gesture
learned of Adam, dwindling
to meanings we no longer know,
but only know our sense of history
has only such barely-touchings, uninterpreted
not-forgettings, to suffice
for its continuance.

The Opportunity

My father once, after his death,
appeared to me as a rose,
passed beyond intellect.
This time, he resumes
human form to become
a boy of six.
I kneel to hug him,
kiss the child's bare shoulder;
near us the ocean
sighs and murmurs,
firm sand reflects
the turn of the wave.

This is my chance to tell him,
'Much has happened, over the years,
many travels.
In the world,
in myself.
Along the way,
I have come to believe
the truth of what you believe.'

The child, with good grace,
permits
my brief embrace; he smiles:
the words
are lazy waves above and around him,
he absorbs their tone,
knows he is loved.
Knows only that.

This was my chance
to speak, I've taken it,
we are both content.

In the language-root place (a wooden
hall, homestead; warm, Homeric, Beowulfian shelter)
candles are glowing, shadows in rhythm
rise and fall. Into this haven have swept,
blown by gusting winds, figures whose drama
makes a stage, for a while, of place and time,
enthralling attention, prompting action,
so that my mind meshes itself in their story
until with promises, tears, laughter, they sweep
out once more into night. Ruefully,
'Life!' I stammer, as the wake of their passage
ebbs and vanishes, 'It rushes and rushes toward me
like Niagara—I don't have time
to write it, to write it down, to hold it, it never
pauses!'   And she whom I address,
the old mother sitting in bed, cheerful, spritely,
cushions behind her, saucer in one hand,
porcelain cup in the other, sipping her fragrant tea,
smiles in wisdom and tells me
that need will pass; she herself
has come to live in what happens, not in the telling.
She quotes to me what a woman
born in slavery said, when she was free and ancient:
I sits here, in my rocker, evenin's,
and just
                purely
                        be's.
The vision
of mighty falls bearing down on me still
thundering in my mind, I see
a crimson candle guttering, flaring, and another, too,
whose wax is an amber yellow almost
the gold of its flame. Colors
of passionate life. I recall

60

Out, out, brief candle. 'Shall I snuff them?' 'Leave them—
they'll still themselves
as the air hushes.'
                    I think of the travellers
gone into dark. 'They were only
passing through,' I say, surprised,
to her, to myself,
relieved and in awe, learning to know
those oncoming waters rushed through the aeons
before me, and rush on beyond me,
and I have now, as the task before me, to *be,*
to arrive at being,
as she the Old Mother has done
in the root place, the hewn
wooden cave, home
of shadow and flame, of
language, gradual stillness,
blessing.

An old man sleeping in the evening train,
face upturned, mouth discreetly closed,
hands clasped, with fingers interlaced.
Those large hands
lie on the fur lining of his wife's coat
he's holding for her, and the fur
looks like a limp dog, docile and affectionate.
The man himself is a peasant
in city clothes, moderately prosperous—
rich by the standards of his youth;
one can read that in his hands,
his sleeping features.
How tired he is, how tired.
I called him old, but then I remember
my own age, and acknowledge he's likely
no older than I. But in the dimension
that moves with us but itself keeps still
like the bubble in a carpenter's level,
I'm fourteen, watching the faces I saw each day
on the train going in to London,
and never spoke to; or guessing
from a row of shoes what sort of faces
I'd see if I raised my eyes.
Everyone has an unchanging age (or sometimes two)
carried within them, beyond expression.
This man perhaps
is ten, putting in a few hours most days
in a crowded schoolroom, and a lot more
at work in the fields; a boy who's always
making plans to go fishing his first free day.
The train moves through the dark quite swiftly
(the Italian dark, as it happens)
with its load of people, each
with a conscious destination, each
with a known age and that other,

the hidden one—except for those
still young, or not young but slower to focus,
who haven't reached yet that state of being
which will become
not a point of arrest but a core
around which the mind develops, reflections circle,
events accrue—a center.
                      A girl with braids
sits in this corner seat, invisible,
pleased with her solitude. And across from her
an invisible boy, dreaming. She knows
she cannot imagine his dreams. Quite swiftly
we move through our lives; swiftly, steadily the train
rocks and bounces onward through sleeping fields,
our unknown stillness
holding level as water sealed in glass.

VI

Witnessing from Afar

Composed by nature, time, human art,
an earthly paradise. A haze that is not smog
gentles the light. Mountains delicately frosted,
timbered autumnal hillsides copper and bronze.
Black-green of pine, gray-green of olive.
Nothing is missing. Ferries' long wakes pattern the water,
send to still shores a minor music of waves.
Dark perpendiculars
of cypress, grouped or single, cross immemorial
horizontals of terraced slopes, the outstretched wings,
creamy yellow, of villas more elegant
in slight disrepair than anything spick and span
ever could be. And all perceived
not through our own crude gaze alone but by the accretion
of others' vision—language, paint, memory transmitted.
Here, just now, the malady
we know the earth endures seems in remission—
or *we* are, from that knowledge that gnaws at us.
But only seems. Down by the lake the sign:
"Swim at your own risk. The lake is polluted."
Not badly, someone says, blithely irrelevant.
We can avoid looking that way,
if we choose. That's at our own risk.
Deep underneath remission's fragile peace,
the misshaped cells remain.

Lago di Como, 1989

Mysterious Disappearance of May's Past Perfect

Even as the beaches blacken again with oil,
reporters tell us, 'If the ship had had
a double hull, the spill
may not have occurred.' And now a poet
writing of one who died some years ago
too young, recounts that had she been and done
otherwise than she was and did, it's thought she
'*may* have survived.' The poet does not agree—
but this impoverished grammar, nonetheless,
places in doubt an undeniable death.
        Is it collective fear suppresses
might have, fear that causes do
produce effects? Does *may* still trail with it,
misused, a comforting openness, illusion
that what has already happened, after all
can be revoked, reversed?
                Or, in these years
when from our mother-tongue some words
were carelessly tossed away, while others hastily
were being invented—chief among them, *overkill*—
has the other meaning, swollen as never before,
of *might* thrust out of memory its minor
homonym, so apt for the precise
nuance of elegy, for the hint of judgement,
reproachful clarities of tense and sense?

The earth is the Lord's, we gabbled,
and the fullness thereof—
while we looted and pillaged, claiming indemnity:
the fullness thereof
given over to us, to our use—
while we preened ourselves, sure of our power,
wilful or ignorant, through the centuries.

Miswritten, misread, that charge:
subdue was the false, the misplaced word in the story.
Surely we were to have been
earth's mind, mirror, reflective source.
Surely our task
was to have been
to love the earth,
to *dress and keep it* like Eden's garden.

That would have been our *dominion:*
to be those cells of earth's body that could
perceive and imagine, could bring the planet
into the haven it is to be known,
(as the eye blesses the hand, perceiving
its form and the work it can do).

They want to be their own old vision
of Mom and Dad. They want their dying son
to be eight years old again, not a gay man,
not ill, not dying. They have accepted him,
they would say if asked, unlike some who shut
errant sons out of house and heart,
and this makes them preen a little, secretly;
but enough of that, some voice within them
whispers, even more secretly, *he's our kid,*
Mom and Dad are going to give him
what all kids long for, a trip to Disney World,
what fun, the best Xmas ever.
And he, his wheelchair strung with bottles and tubes,
glass and metal glittering in winter sun,
shivers and sweats and tries to breathe as *Jingle Bells*
pervades the air and his mother, his father,
chatter and still won't talk, won't listen,
will never listen, never give him
the healing silence
in which they could have heard
his questions, his answers,
his life at last.

The Batterers

A man sits by the bed
of a woman he has beaten,
dresses her wounds,
gingerly dabs at bruises.
Her blood pools about her,
darkens.

Astonished, he finds he's begun
to cherish her. He is terrified.
Why had he never
seen, before, what she was?
What if she stops breathing?

Earth, can we not love you
unless we believe the end is near?
Believe in your life
unless we think you are dying?

Sinister wreathing mist in midsummer sky
slowly disperses
as it descends
over the wooded hill, the lake, the bathing children:

streaks of exhaust left by Blue Angels as they
scream back and forth, virtuosos of costly power,
swifter than hurricane—

to whom a multitude
gazes upward, craving
a violent awe, numb to all else.

So many men—and not the worst of them,
the brutally corrupt, no, others,

liberal, intelligent if not
notably imaginative,

men with likeable eyes—

have mouths that are weak, cruel, twisted,
alien to desire:

mouths that don't match their eyes.

And our wretched history
utters through those mouths

the perfidies their hurt eyes evade.

Living on the rim
of the raging cauldron, disasters

witnessed but
not suffered in the flesh.

The choice: to speak
or not to speak.
We spoke.

Those of whom we spoke
had not that choice.

At every epicenter, beneath
roar and tumult,

enforced:
their silence.

All my life hoping the nightmare
I dreamed as a child (and could make recur
if perverse fascination willed it)
was not prophetic:
              all the animals
seated in peaceful council by candleglow
in a shadowy, fragrant barn,
timeless, unmenaced—then without warning,
without any flash or noise,
the crumbling to black ash, ash
corrugated, writhing, as filmy shreds
of paper used to when sheets of it,
placed round the firescreen to coax the draft
upward and liven the coals, would themselves
catch fire and float, newsprint curdling,
dreadfully out from the hearth towards me.
All my life hoping; having to hope
because decades brought no reassurance.

They have refined the means of destruction,
abstract science almost visibly shining,
it is so highly polished. Immaterial weapons
no one could ever hold in their hands
streak across darkness, across great distances,
threading through mazes to arrive
at targets that are concepts—

But one ancient certainty
remains: war
means blood spilling from living bodies,
means severed limbs, blindness, terror,
means grief, agony, orphans, starvation,
prolonged misery, prolonged resentment and hatred and guilt,
means all of these multiplied, multiplied,
means death, death, death and death.

The children have been practicing,
  diligent before their screens, playing
    a million missions a week.
A few teddybears, cuddly tigers, unicorns,
  still lie prone
    on youthbed pillows.
In antique-shops
  you may find sometimes
    a few small bows and arrows,
  Arthurian picturebooks,
    even cardboard theaters with cut-out
fairytale characters—
  Aladdin, Rose Red, Rose White—
    saved by chance from the garbage;
but the children
  don't even know such things
    gave pleasure once, and are gone.
They're busy with the new
  play-learning: they may not know
    the words *millenium, apocalypse,*
but the expensive games are already
  putting them ahead:
    pilots today, a spokesman says,
have attained
  new speeds of reflex,
    though trained on earlier models.
These children
  are preparing,
    being prepared.
But before their war
  begins,
    others, in which
their brothers, their young fathers
  will be deployed,

may have *taken out*
    the world.
        Perhaps someone
should tell the children, interrupt
    their wasted time?
        Persuade them to run
outdoors for a while, and take
    a look at the unfamiliar
        while it is there—
sky, tree, bird? Or even
    risk their annoyance and
        turn off the power?

They speak of the art of war,
but the arts
draw their light from the soul's well,
and warfare
dries up the soul and draws its power
from a dark and burning wasteland.
When Leonardo
set his genius to devising
machines of destruction he was not
acting in the service of art,
he was suspending
the life of art
over an abyss,
as if one were to hold
a living child out of an airplane window
at thirty thousand feet.

Witnessing from Afar the New Escalation of Savage Power

She was getting old, had seen a lot,
knew a lot.
But something innocent
enlivened her,
upheld her spirits.
She tended a small altar,
kept a candle shielded there,
or tried to. There was a crash and throb
of harsh sound audible
always, but distant.
She believed
she had it in her
to fend for herself and hold
despair at bay.
Now when she came to the ridge and saw
the world's raw gash
reopened, the whole world
a valley of steaming blood,
her small wisdom
guttered in the uprush;
rubbledust, meatpulse—
darkness and the blast
levelled her. (Not her own death,
that was not yet.) The deafening
downrush. Shock, shame
no memory, no knowledge
nor dark imagination
had prepared her for.

January—March 1991

News Report, September 1991
U.S. BURIED IRAQI SOLDIERS ALIVE IN GULF WAR

*"What you saw was a
bunch of trenches with
arms sticking out."*
"Plows mounted on
tanks. Combat
earthmovers."
"Defiant."
"Buried."
"Carefully planned and
rehearsed."
*"When we
went through there wasn't
anybody left."*
"Awarded
Silver Star."
"Reporters
banned."
"Not a single
American killed."
"Bodycount
impossible."
*"For all I know,
thousands,* said
Colonel Moreno."
*"What you
saw was a bunch of
buried trenches
with people's
arms and things
sticking out."*
"Secretary Cheney
made no mention."
"Every single American
was inside

81

the juggernaut
impervious
to small-arms
fire." *"I know
burying people
like that sounds
pretty nasty,* said
Colonel Maggart,
But . . . ."
"His force buried
about six hundred
and fifty
in a thinner line
of trenches."
*"People's arms
sticking out."*
"Every American
inside."
"The juggernaut."
*"I'm not
going to sacrifice
the lives
of my soldiers,*
Moreno said, *it's not
cost-effective."*
*"The tactic was designed
to terrorize,*
Lieutenant Colonel Hawkins
said, who helped
devise it."
"Schwartzkopf's staff
privately
estimated fifty to seventy
thousand killed
in the trenches."
"Private Joe Queen was
awarded
a Bronze Star for burying

trenches with his
earthmover."
"Inside
the juggernaut."
"Impervious."
"A *lot of the guys
were scared,* he said,
*but I
enjoyed it.*"
"*A bunch of
trenches. People's
arms and things
sticking out.*"
"*Cost-effective.*"

In California During the Gulf War

Among the blight-killed eucalypts, among
trees and bushes rusted by Christmas frosts,
the yards and hillsides exhausted by five years of drought,

certain airy white blossoms punctually
reappeared, and dense clusters of pale pink, dark pink—
a delicate abundance. They seemed

like guests arriving joyfully on the accustomed
festival day, unaware of the year's events, not perceiving
the sackcloth others were wearing.

To some of us, the dejected landscape consorted well
with our shame and bitterness. Skies ever-blue,
daily sunshine, disgusted us like smile-buttons.

Yet the blossoms, clinging to thin branches
more lightly than birds alert for flight,
lifted the sunken heart

even against its will.
                    But not
as symbols of hope: they were flimsy
as our resistance to the crimes committed

—again, again—in our name; and yes, they return,
year after year, and yes, they briefly shone with serene joy
over against the dark glare

of evil days. They *are*, and their presence
is quietness ineffable—and the bombings *are*, were,
no doubt will be; that quiet, that huge cacophany

simultaneous. No promise was being accorded, the blossoms
were not doves, there was no rainbow. And when it was claimed
the war had ended, it had not ended.

In the Land of Shinar

Each day the shadow swings
round from west to east till night overtakes it, hiding
half the slow circle. Each year
the tower grows taller, spiralling
out of its monstrous root-circumference, ramps and colonnades
mounting tier by lessening tier the way a searching
bird of prey wheels and mounts the sky, driven
by hungers unsated by blood and bones.
And the shadow lengthens, our homes nearby are dark
half the day, and the bricklayers, stonecutters, carpenters bivouac
high in the scaffolded arcades, further and further above the ground,
weary from longer and longer comings and goings. At times
a worksong twirls down the autumn leaf of a phrase, but mostly
                              we catch
only the harsher sounds of their labor itself, and that seems only
an echo now of the bustle and clamor there was long ago
when the fields were cleared, the hole was dug, the foundations laid
with boasting and fanfares, the work begun.
The tower, great circular honeycomb, rises and rises and still
                              the heavens
arch above and evade it, while the great shadow engulfs
more and more of the land, our lives
dark with the fear a day will blaze, or a full-moon night defining
with icy brilliance the dense shade, when all the immense
weight of this wood and brick and stone and metal and massive
weight of dream and weight of will
will collapse, crumble, thunder and fall,
fall upon us, the dwellers in shadow.

VII

The Almost-Island

One December Night . . .

This I had not expected:
the moon coming right into my kitchen,
the full moon, gently bumping
angles of furniture,
seeming to like the round table
but not resenting corners.

Somehow the moon
filled all the space and yet
left room for whatever
was there already, including me,
and for movement. Like a balloon,
the moon stirred at a breath
and unlike a balloon did not
rise to the ceiling, but wandered
as if sleep-walking,
no more than a foot from the floor.

Music accompanied this lunar visitation—
you would imagine harp or lute, but no,
I'd say it was steel drums,
played with an airy whispering touch.
(Those scooped concavities
might serve as moon-mirrors.)
The greenish tint of white spider-chrysanthemums
resembled the moon's color,
but that was lighter, lighter.

I have been given much, but why this also?
I was abashed. What grand gesture of welcome
was I to make? I bowed, curtsied, but the modest moon
appeared unaware of homage.
I breathed, I gazed; and slowly, mildly,
the moon hovered, touring stove and cupboards,
bookshelves and sink, glimmering
over a bowl of tangerines. And gently
withdrew, just as I thought to summon courage
to offer honey-mead or slivovitz.

Myopic Birdwatcher

One day the solitary heron,
so tall, so immobile on his usual post,
seemed to have shrunk and grown darker.
Had I imagined
his distinction? Now,
when I wanted my friend to see
what I had seen, it was gone.
And the changed heron had two companions,
somber and hunkered down on neighboring posts.

On succeeding days I saw him again
with and without his doubles,
but even alone he looked shabby, fidgetty,
almost sinister, diminished.
I thought it perhaps a matter
of winter plumage,
seasonal behavior.
Till another friend
came with me to the shore.
'Cormorants,' he said.

It lightened my spirits. My heron's place was usurped,
he disdains to return till they leave—
and they may not leave;
but at least I know
it's not he who,
shrugging his wings to dry them
(a vulgar gesture,
though required, it seems,
by cormorant feathers) displays
the high-shouldered baleful silhouette
of Teutonic eagles on old postage-stamps,
black on a sallow ground
of winter lake-light.
At least I know

I didn't deceive myself:
my absent heron's air of austere dignity
was real, whatever hunger
sustains his watchfulness.

Etherial mountain,
snowwhite foam hovering
far above blue, cloudy ridges—
can one believe you are not a mirage?

When my friend drove up the mountain
it changed itself into a big
lump of land with lots of snow on it
and slopes of arid scree.
Another friend climbed it the hard way:
exciting to stay the course, get to the top—
but no sense of height there, nothing to see but
generic mist and snow.
As for me,
when my photos come back developed,
there's just the lake, the south shore of the lake,
the middle distance. No mountain.
                How clearly it speaks! *Respect, perspective,*
privacy, it teaches. *Indulgence*
of curiosity increases
ignorance of the essential.
What does it serve to insist
on knowing more than that a mountain,
forbearing—so far—from volcanic rage,
blesses the city it is poised above, angelic guardian
at rest on sustaining air; and that its vanishings
are needful, as silence is to music?

White as cloud above
a less-white band of cloud
the mountain
stands clear on a sky of
palest blue,
no other clouds in all
the sunny arch
of summer's last holiday.
And the mountain's
deep clefts and hollows,
the shadowy crevasses,
are that same
palest blue, as if
snow and rock,
the whole great mass of mountain,
were transparent
and one could look
through at more sky
southward.
Luminous mountain,
real, unreal sky.

Today the white mist that is weather
is mixed with the sallow tint
of the mist that is smog.
And from it, through it, breathes
a vast whisper:
the mountain.

Sometimes the mountain
is hidden from me in veils
of cloud, sometimes
I am hidden from the mountain
in veils of inattention, apathy, fatigue,
when I forget or refuse to go
down to the shore or a few yards
up the road, on a clear day,
to reconfirm
that witnessing presence.

Tired and hungry, late in the day, impelled
to leave the house and search for what
might lift me back to what I had fallen away from,
I stood by the shore waiting.
I had walked in the silent woods:
the trees withdrew into their secrets.
Dusk was smoothing breadths of silk
over the lake, watery amethyst fading to gray.
Ducks were clustered in sleeping companies
afloat on their element as I was not
on mine. I turned homeward, unsatisfied.
But after a few steps, I paused, impelled again
to linger, to look North before nightfall—the expanse
of calm, of calming water, last wafts
of rose in the few high clouds.
And was rewarded:
the heron, unseen for weeks, came flying
widewinged toward me, settled
just offshore on his post,
took up his vigil.
                If you ask
why this cleared a fog from my spirit,
I have no answer.

Zones of flickering
               water-diamonds
converse with almost-still
      glint of leaves along the poplar-row.

A dispersed array of water-birds relaxes
      afloat in autumn light,
one or another sometimes
               diving casually.

             And far across
        near the other shore,
    the lake is wearing a narrow, trembling
  band of silver,
a silver barely tinged with gold,
delicate tarnish.

        Someone's tapedeck booms and yells
        crescendo . . .
        pulses by and zooms
        out of the park.

        And quiet resumes,
        holding off as best it can
        peripheral sounds of human action—
        planes, subliminal traffic,
        (only one motorboat yet,
        it's a workday morning)—

        but admits
      the long and distant old-time wail of a train:
this quiet, this autumn sun,
        cool air and pale
        diaphanous light,
are generous.

99

Coots, heads bobbing, forever urging themselves
fussily onward . . . How strong their neck-muscles
must be! One is put in mind of human philistines
toiling and spinning through their lives
anxiously complacent in pursuit of trivia.
But coots without warning effortlessly
dive, leaving barely a crease on the black polished-satin
surface—vanishing
into the primal element—!
                                        That gesture
of absolute abandon, absolute
release into clear or cloudy
inner flow of the lake: it's what
artists and mystics want to attain, abjuring
acquisition, drunk on occasional
intuitions, on the sense that
depth, height, breadth don't express the dimension
which invites them, which evades them . . .
(Though mystics desire submersion
to transform them, as it does not transform
the coots, who resume
their pushing and nodding forward
after each plunge. And artists
want not themselves transformed
but their work. The plunge itself
their desire, a way to be
subsumed, consumed utterly
into their work.)

The Almost-Island

The woods which give me their silence,
their ancient Douglas firs and red cedars, their ferns,
are not the wilderness. They're contained
in the two-mile circumference of an almost-island,
a park in city limits. Pleasure-boats crowd at weekends
into the small bay. The veils hiding the mountain
are not always natural cloud. Eagle and heron
speak of solitude, but when you emerge from forest shade
the downtown skyline rears up, phantasmagoric but near,
across the water. Yet the woods, the lake,
the great-winged birds, the vast mountain at the horizon,
are Nature: metonymy of the spirit's understanding
knows them to be a concentrate
of all Thoreau or Wordsworth knew by that word,
Nature: 'a never-failing principle
of joy and purest passion.' Thoreau's own pond
was bounded by the railroad, punctuated
by the 'telegraph trees' and their Aeolian wires.
All of my dread and all of my longing hope that Earth
may outwit the huge stupidity of its humans,
can find their signs and portents here, their recapitulations
of joy and awe. This fine, incised two inches
of goldsmith-work just drifted down, can speak
as well for *tree* as a thousand forest acres,
and tree means depth of roots, uprisen height, outreaching branches.
This musical speech of wavelets jounced against reeds
as a boat's wake tardily reaches the shore,
is *voice of the waters,* voice of all the blue
encircling the terrestrial globe
which as a child I loved to spin
slowly upon its creaking axis—blue globe
we have seen now, round, small as an apple,
afloat in the wilderness we name
so casually, as if we knew it
or ever could know it, 'Space.'

101

VIII

The Tide

Once we've laboriously
disconnected our old conjunctions—
'physical,' 'solid,' 'real,' 'material'—freed them
from antique measure to admit what,
even through eyes not naked but robed
in optic devices, is not perceptible (oh,
precisely is not perceptible!): admitted
that 'large' and 'small' are bereft
of meaning, since not matter but process, process only,
gathers itself to appear
knowable: *world, universe* –

then what we feel
in moments of bleak arrest,
panic's black cloth falling
over our faces, over our breath,

is a new twist of Pascal's dread,
a shift of scrutiny,
                    its object now
inside our flesh, the *infinite spaces* discovered
within our own atoms, inside the least
particle of what we supposed
our mortal selves (and *in* and *out*side,
what are they?)—its object now

bits of the Void left over from before
the Fiat Lux, immeasurably
incorporate in our discarnate, fictive,
(yes, but sentient,) notion of substance,
inaccurate as our language,
flux which the soul alone
pervades, elusive but persistent.

Three hours wholly absorbed: trying to identify one rainsoaked
wormridden mushroom. And the ducks—bufflehead or goldeneye?

The markings once clearly recognized, a glow or grace clarifies
other matters of doubt. They dive, resurface, I know their name.

'What's the most useful thing I can do for you?' I asked the old poet,
lost and distraite in a new apartment. 'Identify things!' she
    answered,

'What are these?' An empty frame. A box of buttons.
An ivory paper knife. For the moment nothing makes sense.

The need to know *maenad* from *dryad,* to know when you see the
    green drift
of watergrass combed by current, the word you desire is *naiad.*

Sorting. Sifting. The ancient tasks, the hero trials, ways to survive,
ways to grow wise. Taxonomies, need to arrange, need to instruct.

We don't trust the stars. *O bright star*—! No, look,
it's moving. Afraid to feel delight.

Tonight two. One was a plane, plodding slowly towards the airport.
One was a star, very silvery. It's still there.

Embracing the Multipede

(I) Embracing the Multipede

On the dream sidewalk
moving towards you
a caterpillar, shiny, hairless, not cute.
Move it
out of harm's way!
It's ringed like an earthworm,
repulsively fecal in color,
with snail-eyes searching about.
Rescue it!
Footsteps will crush it!
It's not so much
like nothing you've seen before
as it is a mixture
of millipede and scorpion.
It's moving towards you,
not cute.
Offer it
your help! It looks
hostile, it may sting you,
but it's small,
each of the multiple feet
the size of an eyelash,
wavering eyes like pinheads.
It's hairless, shiny, repulsive,
scoop it carefully
into your hands,
take it to safety! Not cute, not cute,
it shrinks as you move to meet it,
don't let it vanish before you have time
to give it your heart, a work of mercy.

Where are you going, you
disgusting creature?

It's rumoured
there's a barn, lady,
outside of town,
where anyone may scuttle.

And what would you do there,
vile one?

I'd meet
fellow vile ones, sir,
we'd scuttle, we'd scuttle,
in safety.

And what else, loathsome worm?

God knows.
God would hide in our midst
and we'd seek him.

Return to my dreams,
little leper of my heart:

I want to know—
who are you?

What is the pitiful, wormish,
dangerously creeping thing

I must protect?
Is this a trick to lure me

under the stones,
under the punkwood crevices,

insect shanties that harbor
you and your boneless kin?

Why did the servile answer
you made to insults

twist in its glistening
exuded track to claim

God as your intimate,
ready to join

your lowly games,
to seek and be found?

'Cherish the mystery,'
(a voice responds)
'the mystery of this metamorphic
apparition.
          Does it insidiously
claim your pity? Give it some,
You can spare it.
               Is it treacherous, malevolent?
Give it the benefit
of your ample doubt. You have
no positive evidence
it bites or stings.
Perhaps it has for you
some message,
a talisman brought from whatever distance
it travelled to arrive
at you, you in particular,
you only.'

          Who was speaking?
The creature
was absent, not one shadow
changed shape to mark its trail. Echo
of words remained, as if halloo, halloo,
were sounding in a tunnel.

Literal minds! Embarrassed humans! His friends
were blushing for Him
in secret; wouldn't admit they were shocked.
They thought Him
petulant to curse me!—yet how could the Lord
be unfair?—so they looked away,
then and now.
But I, I knew that
helplessly barren though I was,
my day had come. I served
Christ the Poet,
who spoke in images: I was at hand,
a metaphor for their failure to bring forth
what is within them (as figs
were *not* within me). They who had walked
in His sunlight presence,
they could have ripened,
could have perceived His thirst and hunger,
His innocent appetite;
they could have offered
human fruits—compassion, comprehension—
without being asked,
without being told of need.
My absent fruit
stood for their barren hearts. He cursed
not me, not them, but
(ears that hear not, eyes that see not)
their dullness, that witholds
gifts *unimagined.*

The tree of knowledge was the tree of reason.
That's why the taste of it
drove us from Eden. That fruit
was meant to be dried and milled to a fine powder
for use a pinch at a time, a condiment.
God had probably planned to tell us later
about this new pleasure.
                              We stuffed our mouths full of it,
gorged on *but* and *if* and *how* and again
but, knowing no better.
It's toxic in large quantities; fumes
swirled in our heads and around us
to form a dense cloud that hardened to steel,
a wall between us and God, Who was Paradise.
Not that God is unreasonable—but reason
in such excess was tyranny
and locked us into its own limits, a polished cell
reflecting our own faces. God lives
on the other side of that mirror,
but through the slit where the barrier doesn't
quite touch ground, manages still
to squeeze in—as filtered light,
splinters of fire, a strain of music heard
then lost, then heard again.

On a Theme by Thomas Merton

'Adam, where are you?'
                       God's hands
palpate darkness, the void
that is Adam's inattention,
his confused attention to everything,
impassioned by multiplicity, his despair.

Multiplicity, his despair;
                       God's hands
enacting blindness. Like a child
at a barbaric fairgrounds—
noise, lights, the violent odors—
Adam fragments himself. The whirling rides!

Fragmented Adam stares.
                       God's hands
unseen, the whirling rides
dazzle, the lights blind him. Fragmented,
he is not present to himself. God
suffers the void that is his absence.

Maybe He looked indeed
much as Rembrandt envisioned Him
in those small heads that seem in fact
portraits of more than a model.
A dark, still young, very intelligent face,
a soul-mirror gaze of deep understanding, unjudging.
That face, in extremis, would have clenched its teeth
in a grimace not shown in even the great crucifixions.
The burden of humanness (I begin to see) exacted from Him
that He taste also the humiliation of dread,
cold sweat of wanting to let the whole thing go,
like any mortal hero out of his depth,
like anyone who has taken a step too far
and wants herself back.
The painters, even the greatest, don't show how,
in the midnight Garden,
or staggering uphill under the weight of the Cross,
He went through with even the human longing
to simply cease, to not be.
Not torture of body,
not the hideous betrayals humans commit
nor the faithless weakness of friends, and surely
not the anticipation of death (not then, in agony's grip)
was Incarnation's heaviest weight,
but this sickened desire to renege,
to step back from what He, Who was God,
had promised Himself, and had entered
time and flesh to enact.
Sublime acceptance, to be absolute, had to have welled
up from those depths where purpose
drifted for mortal moments.

114

Stretching Himself as if again,
        through downpress of dust
                upward, soil giving way
to thread of white, that reaches
        for daylight, to open as green
                leaf that it is . . .
Can Ascension
        not have been
                arduous, almost,
as the return
        from Sheol, and
                back through the tomb
into breath?
        Matter reanimate
                now must relinquish
itself, its
        human cells,
                molecules, five
senses, linear
        vision endured
                as Man—
the sole
        all-encompassing gaze
                resumed now,
Eye of Eternity.
        Relinquished, earth's
                broken Eden.
Expulsion,
        liberation,
                last
self-enjoined task
        of Incarnation.
                He again

Fathering Himself.
    Seed-case
        splitting,
He again
    Mothering His birth:
        torture and bliss.

Where is the Giver to whom my gratitude
rose? In this emptiness
there seems no Presence.

•

How confidently the desires
of God are spoken of!
Perhaps God wants
something quite different.
Or nothing, nothing at all.

•

Blue smoke from small
peaceable hearths ascending
without resistance in luminous
evening air.
Or eager mornings — waking
as if to a song's call.
Easily I can conjure
a myriad images
of faith.
Remote. They pass
as I turn a page.

•

Outlying houses, and the train's   rhythm
slows, there's a signal box,
People are taking their luggage
down from the racks.
Then you wake and discover
you have not left
to begin the journey.

•

Faith's a tide, it seems, ebbs and flows responsive
to action and inaction.
Remain in stasis, blown sand
stings your face, anemones
shrivel in rock pools no wave renews.
Clean the littered beach, clear
the lines of a forming poem,
the waters flood inward.
Dull stones again fulfill
their glowing destinies, and emptiness
is a cup, and holds
the ocean.

I had grasped God's garment in the void
but my hand slipped
on the rich silk of it.
The 'everlasting arms' my sister loved to remember
must have upheld my leaden weight
from falling, even so,
for though I claw at empty air and feel
nothing, no embrace,
I have not plummetted.

Notes